Pigeon
Cubes

Pigeon
Cubes

And Other Verse

N. M. Bodecker

ILLUSTRATED BY THE AUTHOR

A MARGARET K. McELDERRY BOOK

Atheneum 1982 *New York*

Library of Congress Cataloging in Publication Data

Bodecker, N. M.
   Pigeon cubes and other verse.

   "A Margaret K. McElderry book."
   Summary: A collection of light verse by the well-known Danish-American author and illustrator.
   1. Humorous poetry, American. 2. Children's poetry, American. [1. Humorous poetry. 2. American poetry]
l. Title.
PS3552.O33P5   811'.54   82–3954
ISBN 0–689–50235–4   AACR2

Copyright © 1982 by N. M. Bodecker   All rights reserved
Published simultaneously in Canada by McClelland & Stewart, Ltd.
Composition by American–Stratford Graphic Services, Inc.
Brattleboro, Vermont
Printed and bound by Fairfield Graphics   Fairfield, Pennsylvania
First Edition

Best of luck to you, dear friend,
from this day 'til all days end.

May your dawns be bright and many;
dandelions few, if any,

where your chancy gardens grow.
There, may all things flourish, so

that before their season closes
your potatoes come up roses.

PIGEON HOLE

No matter what
dread odds you face,
let no one put you
in your place.

The place they pick,
as fit and true,
will make a human
cube of you,

a joyless shape
not only numbing
but naturally
unbecoming.

For nature favors
freer ways:
wide open skies,
unbounded days.

A ready wing,
a questing soul,
unsuited for
a pigeon hole.

And so, my friend,
if you be fond
and dream of days
less cubicund,

come, cross the wires!
Blow the tube!
It's not too late
to fly the cube.

SENSIBLE SUE

This is the story
of sensible Sue
who did nothing whatever
that she shouldn't do,

but ate sensible foods
and wore sensible shoes,
went early to bed
and paid all her dues,

wore rain hats on wet days,
and sun hats on hot,
and when asked: "Do you drink?"
said: "Decidedly not!"

In this sensible manner
so wisely begun
she lived to the age
of one hundred and one,

When they said to her: "Sue, dear,
you must have had fun,"
she replied: "Are you kiddin'?
I never had none!"

and since she'd forgotten
just how to say: "When,"
then blithely went on
to one hundred and ten.

TRUSTWORTHINESS

In God
we trust,
no doubt
or fuss.

The question
is:
does HE
trust US?

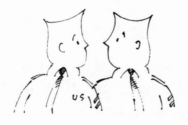

TRAFFIC RULE I

One traffic rule
we all obey:
*the Mack truck has
the right of way.*

RAIN IN THE CITY

First the clouds came,

then the rain,

now the sky is clear again.

I was watching from the curbside
trying vainly to explain:

in this vast, but wasted, effort
all God's clouds went down the drain.

SINGLE

I gather from
the loneliness
that spoils my cherished onlyness,
that hermitry
is not for me,
if I'm deprived of company.
And yet I need,
I must confess,
this solitude. And so I guess
the thing for me
ideally
would be a hermit colony.

UP NORTH

When spring gales,
'round Easter,
northern Maine
pester,
the prudent
down-easter
wears
a sou'-wester.

SIGNS

I always did,
as best I could,
do what the signs
demand I should.

The sign said: STOP.
It saw me stopping.

NO STANDING. Good.
I practiced hopping.

But found initially
perplexing
these wretched signs
inscribed: PEDXING.

"PEDX indeed!" I thought.
"What next?"

Then quite successfully
pedxed!

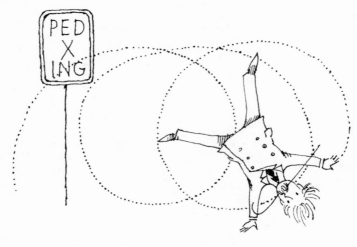

And re-pedxed!
There's nothing to it,
I mean the best
of us can do it.

But still, who would
expect of me
such feats of
pedxterity?

GOOD EGG

Nothing is more honest
than an egg,
it's God's own thing:
the beginning
and the end
of truth in packaging.

GOOD CHEW

People
chew Wrigley's,
but
robins
chew wigglies.

DEVELOPMENT

Step one:
Acquire a small, choice plot of nature.

Step two:
Remove said nature from your plot.

Step three:
Burn brush. Have fun. Roast things in fire.

Step four:
Boil tar. Hot stuff! Make parking lot.

Step five:
Post signs. Chase kids. Have words with neighbor.

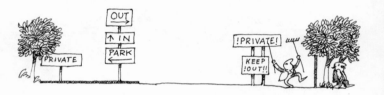

Step six:
Wax wroth. Wave things. Build fence of spite.

Step seven:
Sulk. Despair of human nature.

Step eight:
Make hole. Blast rock. Oh joy! Use dynamite!

Step nine:
Clean up. Oh well. Consult agenda.
Check plans. Have doubts. Call Mom collect.

Step ten:
Build split-Colonial-French-ranch-type-hacienda

and then call in a landscape architect. . . .

NUMBER TWO

No matter what
I try to do
I'm always only
number two.

The runner-up's complaint,
I guess:
I'M TRYING HARDER
—but with less success.

CITYSCAPE

I watch the new city,
impersonal, gray.
Not simple carelessness
made it that way.

It sprang from the souls
of the powers that be
who do take their ugliness
seriously.

And that lends a certain
perverted *noblesse*
to this almost fastidious
hideousness.

GLOIRE

In Avenue Victor Hugo
she said, I thought *mal à propos:*
"You may observe, my jaded gem,
some men have streets named after them.

But when we passed, in Rue du Bac,
a modest lane marked: *Cul de Sac*
I said with pride: "My dear, you see
they also named a street for me."

SPRING MORNING IN
BOSTON'S SOUTH END

In the middle
of the garbage
in a littered yard,
a tulip,
catching rain
and sun
and odors
in a blessed,
pungent
julep.

Proving what?
That life is stronger?
Beauty tough
as anything?
Or perhaps
that in the garbage
life is rich
and nourishing?
Well, whatever
may have prompted
this one tulip's
silent fling,
thank you kindly
for upholding
even here
the rights of spring.

GLASS WALLING

When searching for
the eye, alas
one faces walls
of one-way glass,
a hostile glint,
a silent shout:
"You who approaches me
Keep Out!"

This blank surveillance,
secret, stark,
that keeps the whole
world in the dark,
what mayhem may
it be akin to?
The eye that hides
wants looking into.

TOWN MEETING *or*
"HEY MAN, DON'T SPEAK SO GOOD"

A dear
old-fashioned
type arose
and spoke
his piece
in perfect
prose.

But no one
grasped
the guy's
complaint;
he was
too sweetly
eloquaint.

IF

If the pie crust
isn't right,
never bake a pie again.

If the tie knot
isn't tight,
never tie a tie again.

If at first
you don't succeed,
never, ever try again.

Just say; "Life
is hard indeed."
And cry, cry and cry again.

D.A.R.

A revolution
looking
for supporters
would have
but scant
success
among
its daughters.

SWEET HISTORY

How fortunate
that things don't last.
The past is nice
because it's past.

Hail history!
Last year's neuralgia,
reborn as this year's
pet nostalgia.

A daughter's to her mother—

a sister's to her brother—

a father's to his business partner Gibbs—

a fiddler's to his fiddle—

a belly dancer's to her middle—

a druggist's to his drugs and nasal drips—

39

a present's to its giver—

a Livonian's to his liver—

all today are "meaningful relationships."

NEW ENGLAND ROAD

Coasting down
a New England road
I came
on this welcoming sign:
"ENTERING MOULTONVILLE
Settled
in sixteen-hundred-and-seventy-nine."
But nothing
happened,
the road
went on,
mile
after
mile
in the autumn sun,
wood lots
and stone walls
and milkweed pods,
New England asters
and golden rods . . .
When all of a sudden,
settlers galore:

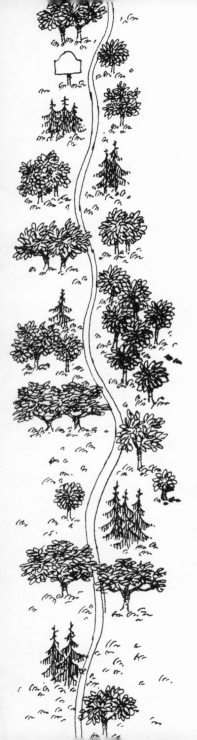

three churches,
two gas tanks,
a country store!
Then nothing further
for miles
but peace,
and rolling
New England country ease,
hemlocks
and maples
and fields,
and then:
the sign,
remember,
from way back when?
"LEAVING MOULTONVILLE
Settled
etc.
Come Again."

JOURNEY'S END

The gas gauge
showed empty,
the journey
was over,
I stretched
in the sun
among daisies
and clover,
cheered by
this innocent
circumlocution:
I didn't run out of gas.
I ran out of pollution!

WINDY DAY

Dependency
is a terrible thing:
pity the kite
in need of its string.

44

AT SUNRISE

It's nothing when I look again:
a drop of moisture on a tree.
But for a moment it was light
that like a small sun glowed at me,

and, brimming with that moment's joy,
bridged all the light years to the sun,
before it knew its proper path.
And gathered weight. And ambled on.

IS IT NICE TO BE WISE?

Age may bring wisdom,
but if I be truthful
experience teaches
that youth is more useful.

BEAUTIFICATION

Beautification
is ideal,
but uglification
is for real.

TERROR

I wake in the grip
of a terminal terror:
THE WORLD WAS CREATED
DUE TO AN ERROR
that cannot much longer
remain undetected,
but any day now
will be firmly corrected.

CITY DAWN

I pulled up the shade
to see the sun rise,
but saw only wakening
blight there,
and a stain in the smog,
like a moon in disguise,
the thing that passes for
light there.
I stared at the city
without much surprise
that they should hold on to the
night there,
for the city stared back
with the million wild eyes
that daily wake up to a
nightmare.

NEW DAY

Mornings bring
both hope
and curses:
God makes
light,
and I make
verses.

THIS LIFE

This life
does some
poor creatures
dirt,
and Mother Nature
lets it:
the early
robin
gets the worm,
the early
worm
just gets it.

BLESSINGS

Spring is the promise,

summer is the kiss,

autumn is bedtime,

and Winter is bliss.

A MATTER OF PRINCIPLE

Their principles
were iron-clad,
their faithfulness
remorseless.
Each sacrificed
a life to stay
defiantly
divorceless.

A SIMPLE NEED

What this country needs
is an old-fashioned plot
with no commercials to spoil it:
a TV set
in every pot,
and instructions on how to boil it.

FLOUNDERING

I am sitting
at the bottom
of the sea;
I am a flounder,
and no one
could be flatter,
less conspicuous
or rounder.

But sometimes
sunny mornings
fill my aging heart
with dread,
when kids
are skipping pebbles
on the ripples
overhead.

Then it's good
to be anonymous,
for why should it
be known
that this old
confounded flounder
loves a bright young
skipping stone?

MORNING AT THE POST OFFICE

This much, I think,
defies debate:
some rhymes are most
unfortunate.

I lick a stamp,
read: U.S. MAIL,
when echoes answer:
"Use a snail."

I feel
(I know it's idiotic)
unspeakably
unpatriotic.

THE AMERICAN DILEMMA
(Once: Small Car Blues)

We could
of course
have made
a car
as small
as *their*
small foreign
star,
had we
not felt
compelled
to figger
a way
to make
our
small car
BIGGER.

NEWBREAD

A loaf of bread
was once a meal
a workman
went to bed on.
It's now a bag
of puffy fluff
a tot could rest its head on.

CRUSTRATION

I am hampered
in my progress
by the meanest
of frustrations:
though the world
could be my oyster
I'm allergic
to crustaceans.

SNAPSHOTS

Year after year
we put away
more snapshots
for a rainy day.

To have and hold
from this day on
each precious, dated
moment gone.

We should accept
with grace (but won't)
that now you see it,
now you don't.

Time's own way
of avoiding glut:
To open briefly—
then snap shut.

KNOW HIM?

I'm not a snob,
I must insist,
and certainly
not prejudiced.

I only wish
that people would
respect my one-man
neighborhood.

BEWARE OF SPEAKER

Beware
the atrocity
of
verbopomposity.

WATER SPORT

To shower at sea
is a curious sport:
the shower moves starboard
when you move to port.

When *you* move to starboard
the shower moves back;
you pass and repass
on the opposite tack,

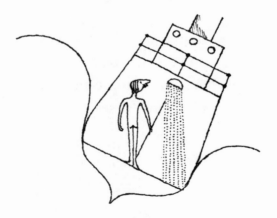

creating the somnam-
bulistic sensation
of uncompromising
mis-synchronization,

from which you must snatch
(oh, infrequent infusions)
your moments of truth
with the passing ablutions,

trapped by the nautical
powers that be
in a metronome-pendulum
syndrome at sea.

AWAKE

When headaches keep
away my sleep
I like to count
two-headed sheep;

it makes me feel
a little better
that they may have
a double-header.

ORBIT'S END

Wayward things
from outer spaces
dropping back
to earthly places,

lighting their
re-entry fires
and consumed
in streaking pyres,

write their timely
commentaries:
fiery
orbituaries.

INDEX

811.54   (FUTURE VINCENT - PERSONAL)
Bo
Bodecker, N.M.
Pigeon cubes and other poems

811.54   (FUTURE VINCENT -PERSONAL
Bo
    Bodecker, N.M.
AUTHOR

TITLE   Pigeon cubes and other poems

DATE LOANED	BORROWER'S NAME	DATE RETURNED